GW00383262

.ET

Third Steps in Ballet

BASIC ALLEGRO STEPS

Thalia Mara

ILLUSTRATED BY LOUISE HOLMGREN

A DANCE HORIZONS BOOK
Princeton Book Company, Publishers
Princeton, New Jersey

Copyright © 1957 by Thalia Mara

All rights reserved. No part of this book may be reproduced or
utilized in any form or by any means, electronic or mechanical,
including photocopying, recording or by any information storage
and retrieval system, without permission in writing from the Publisher.

Reprinted 1987 Princeton Book Company, Publishers
P.O. Box 109
Princeton, NJ 08542

This is an unabridged republication of the first edition published
in 1957 by Garden City Books, Garden City, N.Y.

ISBN 916622-55-X

Library of Congress Catalog Card Number 70-181475

Printed in the United States of America

FOREWORD: TO PARENTS

Like its predecessors, *First Steps in Ballet* and *Second Steps in Ballet*, this book has as its purpose a clear and simple exposition of certain aspects of ballet technique so that the elementary ballet student may practice intelligently and correctly, at home, the steps and exercises that are being learned in the classroom. It is not intended, in any way, to supplant the teacher. On the contrary, its purpose is to aid the teacher by making students more aware of the importance of correct understanding of the details of technique. I state again, unequivocally, that the study of ballet must not be undertaken except under the guidance of a really able and competent teacher.

The average ballet student in our country, even one with professional aspirations, finds it difficult to attend more than one, two, or at most three ballet classes per week. The pressure of schoolwork and other normal activities as well as the mother's time and the necessity of either chauffering or traveling with the youngsters are the usual reasons for this minimum study, although the economic factor plays a large part too.

Two or three hours per week is really very little time to devote to an art as exacting and demanding as ballet. If the young student wishes to make real progress (particularly if the youngster dreams of making a career in ballet), there must be much thought given to the work outside the classroom. Ballet is just as mental as it is physical. In order to perform the movements and steps of ballet correctly and with grace, ease, and form the student must first form the correct mental concept and then endeavor to make the body conform to the demands made upon it by the movement or step.

Just as *First Steps* and *Second Steps* were designed to give the elementary student a clear understanding of the most basic exercises at the barre and in center practice, so this book is intended to make clear the most basic jumping and connecting steps of ballet. The student who understands the technical details of these steps will certainly perform them better, and, since the more complicated steps are based upon the correct execution of these basic steps, this will lay the foundation for better dancing.

Parents often give teachers a very hard time because of their lack of comprehension as to what the art of ballet is and of what its proper study should consist. Unfortunately, the conscientious teacher often seems to suffer more from this than the unscrupulous one. So many mothers are under the false impression that progress in ballet consists of constantly learning "something new." They feel that the child must learn new steps and new dances each year. Teachers are often accused of holding back a student because the new steps and dances are 5 not forthcoming.

True progress in ballet is made very slowly and consists not of new steps and dances but rather of repetition of the basic exercises, steps, and movements to acquire the strength, muscle tone, and correct body placement needed in ballet. By painstaking care the teacher and student together are fashioning a dance instrument just as the craftsman fashions a fine musical instrument with his tools and basic materials. Pushing a child into more advanced steps before those already taught have been properly assimilated retards true progress rather than hastening it.

"But," you may say, "I am not interested in having my child become a professional dancer. I only want her to acquire a little grace, some poise, and better posture." All the more reason then, mother, to be happy that your child's teacher is conscientious enough to work painstakingly and carefully to develop more control and more strength in your child. For it is precisely this that gives your child the benefits you are demanding. The conscientious teacher deserves your complete confidence and support. Beware of the teacher who is always teaching "new" and more advanced work without regard to the individual child's response and physical development. This, of course, is not to say that the work in the classroom should be dull and unvaried. On the contrary, the good teacher is always varying the exercises to develop mental agility in the child as well as to maintain the child's interest.

Ambitious mothers often seem to feel that there is a stigma attached to being in a lower ballet grade. I sometimes wonder if they have the same mental attitude toward their children's academic schooling. It is interesting to note that the practice of pushing school children ahead from grade to grade, regardless of their ability to pass, is now being condemned, by educators and by parents alike, as being of inestimable harm to children in their mental development. The same is surely true of ballet and the physical development of the child.

The best advice that I, or any other good teacher, can give you is to select your child's ballet teacher with care, being governed only by the desire to find an able and capable teacher of good balletic background and not by considerations of location or price. Then, having selected and placed your child in the school of your choice, express your confidence in the teacher by accepting her (or his) decisions as to what your child is capable of doing. Realize that the teacher has no desire to hold any student back and no ulterior motive in so doing. This is not to the teacher's advantage any more than it is to the student's.

Remember, too, that some children are phlegmatic or naturally lazy physically and the effort of using the muscles of the body is distasteful to them. The conscientious teacher who is trying to give you your money's worth by helping the child to better posture through the strengthening regime of exercise (for it takes a great deal of strength in the postural muscles to aid the child in standing straight) has a much harder job with such a child than with one who is enthusiastic over exercise and who is physically ambitious. There are varying degrees of aptitude, too, to be considered. I use the word "aptitude" rather than "talent" for real dance talent does not begin to show until after several years of training.

Remember, then, that you, as a layman, are no real judge of your child's ability and that your child's reaction to lessons may be determined by natural laziness and the lack of desire to make the real physical effort required by good training. The teacher, who is an expert, is the only real judge of what your child should be doing.

Most children, even those who lack real aptitude and the physical attributes for dancing, develop a love for their lessons and enthusiasm for their work. I believe that this is caused, in large part, by the challenge that good training presents to them and to their feeling of achievement when they accomplish the mastery of a step or exercise.

The tendency, today, to make everything easy for the developing child is certainly no boon to that child. The habits of concentration, perseverance, and the ability to face up to challenging problems by meeting and overcoming them must be formed in childhood. One reason that exposure to ballet is so good for children is that ballet is such a highly disciplined art. The child learns to discipline both the body and the mind—something that stands us all in good stead in adult life.

Thalia Mara

ADVICE TO STUDENTS

This little book is concerned with that part of ballet class that so many of you students seem to enjoy the most. These are the basic elevation and connecting steps of ballet. By "elevation" we mean steps that are taken off the ground by leaping or springing. It is natural that this should be a favorite part of class, for the basic steps of ballet are to the dance what words are to a language. With these steps we make "enchainements" (ahn-shenn-mahng'), or "combinations." That is, we put them together, in a series, in various combined forms to develop balletic phrases and sentences just as we put words together to form sentences in speech.

In order to perform these basic steps well—that is, with ease, control, and balletic form—much strength is needed in the feet, legs, and back.

Balletic form means that when you leave the ground in a leaping or springing step you are able to point your feet, turn your legs well outward, hold your back very straight, hold your arms gracefully in a given position, control your head in a given position, and exhibit good "line" in your poses in the air.

Ease means that while you are doing all of these things you do not show any strain by hunching your shoulders, straining your neck cords, or tensing your arms or hands.

Control means that you are able to jump to the necessary height and then alight gracefully, softly, and lightly on the ground without any loss of posture or poise.

Now you can readily see that, in order to perform the steps of allegro correctly, there must be much preliminary work in order to develop the strength needed. This strength must be developed first through consistent practice of the exercises of barre work. That is the function of the barre exercises—to develop the strength you need in your feet, legs, and back and to make your tendons and muscles elastic and springy. These same exercises must also be practiced away from the barre in order to develop your sense of balance.

Now, let us say that you have been practicing your barre work faithfully and that you have also been practicing your center barre and adagio exercises. You are progressing in your classwork and you are eager to practice, at home, the steps and little combinations of steps your teacher is now giving you in the classroom.

There are two parts to your allegro practice. The first is to practice each step individually for perfection of execution. This is very important in itself, for in an enchainement, or combination, each step must be as perfect as a little jewel in order for the effect to be as sparkling as *allegro* dancing demands. The second part is to work on the *enchaînements* given you by your teacher. This is important to develop your memory powers so that you can connect one step to another easily. The ability to do this comes from being able to think one step ahead each time, and, to do this, the mind must be made more quick and agile by exercising thought just as you do your muscles.

But, at this point, I must ask you to pay particular attention to what follows: NEVER practice these jumping steps without first "warming up" the muscles and tendons of your legs and feet by at least fifteen or twenty minutes of good barre work. Start with *pliés*, proceed to *battements tendus* and *dégagés*, finish up with *grands battements* and *relevés* to get your muscles toned up and your tendons stretched. Work carefully and slowly. Trying to jump with "cold" legs and feet may cause you to injure yourself seriously by twisting or spraining your ankle or fore-foot or damaging the Achilles' tendon, which is at the back of your ankle and heel. No professional dancer would dream of practicing *allegro* or dancing on the stage without this preliminary warm-up of barre practice. You, too, must be guided by the wisdom and experience of the professional dancer.

In practicing the steps remember that your arms, your shoulders, and your head are a very important part of your equipment as a dancer. Here is where all our practice of *port de bras*, *épaulement*, and directions of the body in space become of practical use. The movements of the arms and hands, the turn of the shoulders and head must be co-ordinated with those of the feet and legs, for they embellish the movement and show the grace of the dancer. Sometimes we merely hold our arms still, but they must be held in a correct position with no tension or strain. At other times we move our arms in co-ordination and harmony with the legs, and they must move gracefully and flowingly, not in stiff, jerky movements. This is most difficult to do well and requires infinite care in practice. The same is true of the head and shoulders. At times we hold the head erect and face directly front; at other times we turn our shoulders to *croisé* or *effacé* and incline the head. This gives variety, interest, and artistic quality to our jumping.

Of course you cannot master everything at once. Begin by getting a good command of the legs and feet, but as soon as possible try to add the arm movements and then the *épaulement*. Remember that it takes many years of striving to achieve the perfection you hope to obtain.

Thalia Mara

CONTENTS

ALLEGRO

Allegro is an Italian word meaning "glad" or "merry." In music it denotes a quick and lively tempo. In ballet it is used as a general term for all of the steps of elevation—that is, jumping steps—which are generally performed to 2/4, 3/4, 4/4, 3/8, or 6/8 rhythm played at a lively tempo. All of the steps described in this book are the simple basic steps of ballet and come under the general term of "allegro."

Another word you need to know well is "*ballon*" (bahlohn'). *Ballon* is an essential part of *allegro* dancing. We speak of a dancer as having "good *ballon*" or as having "no *ballon*." *Ballon* in ballet means a bouncy quality in jumping. It means that the dancer bounds up from the floor, stays a moment in the air, and alights from the jump with lightness and elasticity like a rubber ball that bounces across the floor. A dancer who has no *ballon* gives the impression of being heavy and bound to the floor, the dancer who has good *ballon* gives the impression of being light and in flight. So, you see, good *ballon* is essential to the dancer.

You must also realize that no dancer is born with good *ballon*, although some people are naturally able to jump higher than others. Good *ballon* is the result of proper technical training. It is achieved through the correct use of the insteps of the feet and the elasticity of the knees and Achilles' tendons.

By studying the next eight pages carefully and then putting into practice the theory explained there you will acquire good *ballon*. Remember that the faithful practice of your barre exercises—*demi-pliés, battements tendus, dégagés,* and *frappés,* as well as *relevés*—is your best aid in acquiring better *ballon* in your jumps.

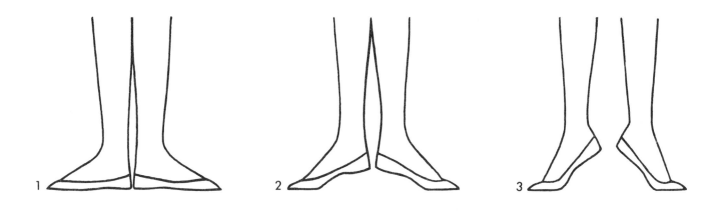

THE VARIOUS LEVELS OF THE FOOT, AND THE ACTION OF THE FOOT IN JUMPING

1. *Pied à terre* (pee-ay' ah tair). The foot "on flat." In springing upward we always begin from a position with the heels or heel pressed firmly against the floor, depending on whether we are springing from two feet or one foot.

2. *Pied à quart* (pee-ay' ah kar'). The foot at Quarter Point. We push away from the floor by forcefully pushing up through the insteps. As we begin this push the heel comes up first.

3. *Pied à demi* (pee-ay' ah deh-mee'). Also called "sur la demi-pointe" (soor lah deh-mee' pwahnt). We continue to push up through the ball of the foot.

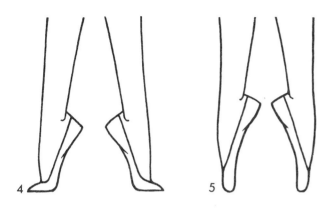

4. *Pied à trois quart* (pee-ay' ah trwah kar). The foot at three-quarter point. We continue to push up through the instep.

5. *Pied à pointe* (pee-ay' ah pwahnt). Also called "*sur la pointe.*" The Full Point Position. In jumping our last contact with the floor is the tips of our toes as we push them downward into a strong point the instant we leave the floor.

In descending from a jump we reverse this action of the foot or feet. The toes remain pointed until almost the instant of contact with the floor (5), the first contact with the floor is high on the three-quarter point (4), we roll down into the under part of the ball of the foot (3), we continue to roll down the metatarsal arch, controlling the descent of the heel (2), we complete the landing with the heel pressed firmly into the floor, all of the toes straight on the floor, the arch well lifted (1).

In working on *adagio* and on turns, as well as in jumping, it is necessary for a dancer to have complete control and balance at any level of the foot shown here. These levels of balance are used in different ways for various purposes. Of course the Full Point Position is the one girls use in "toe dancing."

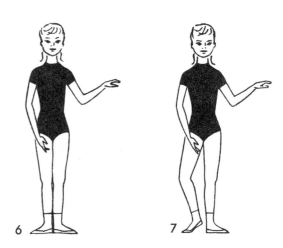

6

7

EXERCISE

Practice this exercise at the barre. It will help you to acquire good *ballon*.

6. Ready to begin. Stand in First Position holding the barre with the left hand. The weight of the body is evenly distributed over both feet. Remember that, in ballet, balance is over the *balls* of the feet so that, although your heels are held firmly against the floor, they do not carry the weight of the body. You should feel as though you could raise the heels off the ground at any time you wish to do so. Think of all the rules of good body placement. Hold the right arm in the Fifth Position Low.

7. Raise your right heel, pushing down into the ball of the foot. Count, "And."

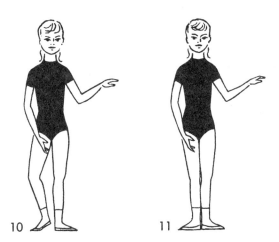

10. Roll down the toes to the ball of the foot. Count, "A."

11. Roll down the instep to the heel, returning the foot to First Position. Allow the weight of the body to equalize itself over both feet. Count, "Two."

Practice this exercise 16 times with the right foot, then turn around and practice it 16 times with the left foot. You may also practice this exercise from Second Position instead of First Position.

8. Roll upward through the toes of the right foot, pushing forcefully against and from the floor until the pointed toes are pointed a few inches above the floor. At the same time transfer the weight of the body to the left foot. (Take care not to sit into your left hip.) Count, "A one."

9. Lower the right foot until the tips of the toes touch the floor. Count, "And."

THE IMPORTANCE OF THE PLIE
IN JUMPING

While it is necessary to acquire the correct action of the insteps of the feet in order to jump lightly and descend softly, the correct use of the feet alone is not sufficient to make us jump well.

The *plié* is of equal importance with the use of the insteps to give lightness and bounce to our leaping and springing steps. Without this springy action of the knees it is impossible to jump high, to bound, or to leap.

Prove it to yourself. Stand on both feet with the knees straight. Now try to jump up off the floor without bending your knees either as you take off or as you land. You see how impossible it is to get any elevation off the ground—and in landing with stiff knees the result is bumpy, jerky, and jarring to the spine.

It is the soft bending of the knees as the heels are lowered to the ground that gives smoothness to our jumping.

The most important part of learning to jump well is to begin a jump with a *demi-plié*, the heels pressed firmly into the floor, and to finish the jump with a *demi-plié*, the heels again pressed firmly into the floor. There are several reasons for the importance of this point.

The Achilles' tendon, which is at the back of the ankle

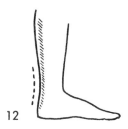

12

at the heel, is a very powerful factor in jumping. If this tendon is not stretched fully, by a good *demi-plié*, each time you begin or end a jump it becomes stiff and thickened instead of elastic and springy. Once it becomes stiff, it is impossible to execute a good *demi-plié* with the heels properly pressed into the floor, and almost impossible ever to stretch it out. The dancer, in such a case, has no real control over the body in landing from a jump because the ankles are wobbly without the firm pressure of the heels against the floor. The ankles may easily be sprained or even broken by such lack of control.

Furthermore, it is this push-off of the heels from the floor that gives the power to jump high, and it is the soft descent into the heels that makes landing light.

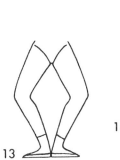
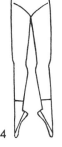

13   14   15

16. Incorrect position in landing from a jump. The knees have been allowed to fall in front of the arches causing the feet to roll in. This will certainly cause damage to the feet as the strain of taking the full weight of the body in landing is too much for the arches in this position.

17. OOF! Don't ever land from a jump with stiff knees.

12. The Achilles' tendon.

13. Preparation for a spring from the floor.

14. Position of the legs and feet in the air. The turn-out must be maintained at the hips and the feet always pointed as soon as they leave the ground.

15. Finish of the jump. Knees pushed back and out directly over the toes. Feet holding the floor with big toe, little toe, and heel.

16   17

19

HOW TO KEEP YOUR JUMPING LIGHT

"Dancers should be seen and not heard." Of course. Nothing is more ridiculous than a dancer who lands heavily and noisily from a jump. A dancer must give the impression of flight—of being air-borne, not earth-bound.

We have already spoken about two things that make jumping light. One is the correct use of the insteps and the other is the correct use of *demi-plié*.

There is another contributing factor to jumping lightly. This is the proper lift of the ribs and the pulling upward of the body out of the hips. In other words, at all times, the weight of the body must be pulled upward and distributed through the body rather than resting entirely upon the feet.

If you have been faithful about working on your posture and body placement, you will have no trouble with this. See *First Steps in Ballet*.

When the landing is made from a jump, the weight of the body must be controlled by this upward lift. If the back is held strong and straight (by lifting the ribs, pulling the shoulder blades down, and keeping the buttocks under), as we touch the floor and roll down into the proper *plié* the landing will be noiseless. If, on the contrary, the back is allowed to weaken and the body to "break" as the landing is made, the result will be noisy even if the insteps, heels, and knees are working properly. Besides it looks dreadful to see such loss of control in the back and spoils the entire artistic effect of the jump.

Proper breathing is another big factor in learning to jump lightly. We dancers must learn breath control just as singers do. The important rule for breathing in jumping is to "breathe with the effort." That is, inhale as you spring upward and expel the air easily and slowly in alighting. The higher the jump the deeper the breath.

The eyes, too, are important in jumping, as is the head. If you want to jump high and look good in the air, keep your chin up and look straight out. Never hang your head. Don't look down at the floor. Keep your shoulders down. Hunching them does not help to get you up higher; it merely makes you look awkward.

Timing is a very important part of jumping too. When the music is slow, we must jump higher than when the music is fast. We, therefore, must be guided by the music in determining how high to jump in any step. If we jump too high and do not keep the tempo, the jump will look heavy no matter how high it is. And, of course, since rhythm is such a basic part of dancing, no one who is unmusical can ever be called a dancer.

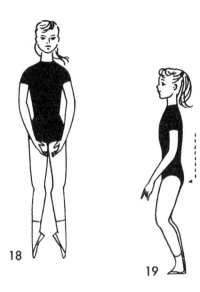

20. Heels off the floor in the preparatory *plié* or in alighting from a jump.

21. Ribs dropped, shoulders hunched, buttocks sticking out, in the air.

22. "Break" in landing, ribs dropped, buttocks sticking out.

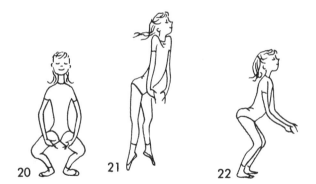

18. In the air keep your back straight by lifting your ribs, pulling your shoulder blades down and under, lifting up out of the hips, and keeping your buttocks under.

19. On the floor, in preparing for a jump and in alighting from a jump, keep your back straight and your buttocks under.

TEMPS LEVÉ ON TWO FEET (tahn leh-vay')

The translation of "*temps levé*" is "elevated time." When the word "*temps*" is used as part of the name of a step, it refers to the preparatory beat of the music before the actual beat. Therefore the name of this step stems from the fact that we are in the air on the preparatory beat finishing on the floor on the actual beat of the music.

Temps levé on two feet may be taken from First Position, Second Position, or Fourth Position.

TEMPS LEVÉ IN FIRST POSITION

23. Ready to begin. Stand erect, feet in First Position, arms in First Position.

24. *Demi-plié*. Remember to keep your head erect and your eyes open, looking straight out. Think of your back. Press your heels firmly into the floor.

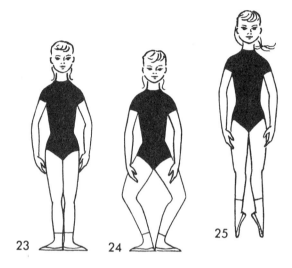

23 24 25

25. Push up off the ground, forcing your knees to straighten and your toes to push down into a strong point. Do not throw your legs apart or bring them together, keep them well turned outward from the hips. Remember to keep your back straight and strong and to keep your buttocks tightened. The arms remain in First Position.

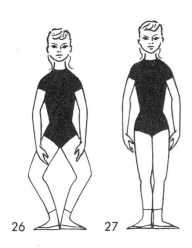

26   27

26. Finish in a good *demi-plié* with both heels pressed firmly into the floor. Your back must be strong as steel! Keep your head up, don't roll in on your arches, press your knees back and out over your toes, don't stick your seat out in back. Remember to touch the floor with the toes first and then to roll down into the heels.

27. Straighten both knees.

Practice the *temps levé* in this manner 8 times. If you are practicing to music, use a 2/4 rhythm. Alight from the jump on the first beat of the measure and straighten the knees on the second beat.

You may also practice this step without straightening the knees between jumps. Hold the *plié* position for the second beat of the measure and spring up into the next *temps levé* from this *plié*. Both ways are valuable for practice. The first way will make you conscious of the action of your knees and the necessity for keeping them springy; the second way will give you time to think of holding the back strong, the knees turned out, the feet straight, and the chin up as you struggle to keep your heels pressed into the floor.

After you have practiced this *temps levé* in First Position, practice it the same way with the feet and the arms in Second Position.

Practice the *temps levé* with the feet in Fourth Position 8 times with the right foot front, 8 times with the left foot front. Hold the arms in Fourth Position High (see *Second Steps in Ballet*) with the raised arm on the side opposite the front foot.

28

29

30

31

TEMPS LEVÉ FROM TWO FEET TO ONE FOOT

DERRIÈRE (deh-ree-air') (in back)

28. Ready to begin. Stand in Fifth Position with the right foot front. Arms in Fifth Position Low.

29. *Demi-plié.*

30. Spring straight up into the air, point both feet, straighten both knees. Arms remain in Fifth Position Low, head erect.

31. Alight on the right foot, rolling down into a *demi-plié* and at the same time raise the left foot *sur le cou de pied derrière* (sur leh coo deh pee-ay') (in back of ankle). At the instant you land raise the left arm to Demi-Seconde Position, and incline the head to the right. Remember, back straight, seat under, all the toes on the floor, heel on the floor, knee well bent and pushed out over the toes, point the left foot strongly and press its heel against the calf muscle of the right leg.

DEVANT (dih-vahn') (in front)

Ready to begin as in Number 8.

32. *Demi-plié.*

33. Spring straight up into the air, point both feet, straighten both knees. Arms remain in Fifth Position Low, head erect.

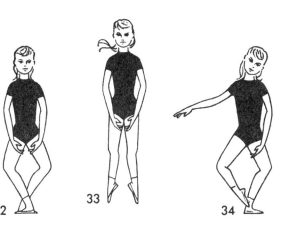

32   33   34

34. Alight on the left foot; at the same time raise the right foot *sur le cou de pied devant* (in front of the left ankle). At the instant you land raise the right arm to Demi-Seconde Position, and incline the head to the left. Hold the right foot close to the left shin-bone and point it strongly.

Practice the *temps levé* from two feet to one foot in combination with the *assemblé* (see page 36). Use a 2/4 rhythm.

Stand in Fifth Position, left foot front. Do a *temps levé*, raising the right foot *sur le cou de pied derrière*, count, "And one." Hold the *plié* position for count "And two." Take an *assemblé dessus* (page 36) with the right foot, count, "And one." Hold the *plié* position for count "And two." Repeat the *temps levé* and the *assemblé* with the left foot. Take the entire step alternating right foot and left 4 times.

Hold the arms in Demi-Seconde Position until you feel sure of the feet and are able to do the steps well, then add the arm movements to your practice.

You may also practice this step in reverse. Take your *temps levé sur le cou de pied devant* and your *assemblé dessous* (page 38).

35

36

37

TEMPS LEVÉ ON ONE FOOT

This *temps levé* may be done with the raised foot held either *sur le cou de pied derrière* or *devant*.

DERRIÈRE

35. Ready to begin. Stand on the right foot in a *demi-plié* with the left foot raised to a pointed position behind the right calf muscle. Remember, hold the floor firmly with the big toe, little toe, and heel, keep the back straight, both knees well turned outward. Hold the left arm in Fifth Position Low and the right arm in Demi-Seconde Position (Cecchetti Third Position); incline the head to the left.

36. Spring straight up into the air, pointing the right foot strongly. Keep the head inclined, the back straight and strong, and the arms in the same position. Count, "And."

37. Come down into a soft *plié* on the right foot rolling down the instep to the heel. Keep your back strong, don't "break." Hold the left foot in its pointed position behind the right calf muscle, press both knees back and out over the toes, retain the position of the arms and the inclination of the head. Count, "One."

DEVANT

38, 39, 40. To execute this *temps levé sur le cou de pied devant*, raise the left foot in front of the right leg at the center of the shinbone. Hold the right arm in Fifth Position Low, the left arm in Demi-Seconde Position and the head inclined to the right.

Practice the *temps levé* on the right foot 8 times with the left foot *sur le cou de pied derrière*. Then practice it 8 times on the left foot with the right foot *sur le cou de pied derrière*. Practice 8 times on each foot with the *cou de pied devant* position. Use a 2/4 rhythm played slowly.

Spring into the air, each time, on the preparatory beat and *plié* well on the actual beat of the music.

You may also practice this *temps levé* in combination with the *jeté* (pages 40 and 42). Use the same 2/4 rhythm. Take a *jeté derrière* ("And one"); *temps levé* with the raised foot *sur le cou de pied derrière* ("And two"). Repeat the *jeté* and *temps levé* on the other foot. Do this combination 8 times. This step will travel forward. You may also travel backward by taking *jeté devant* and your *temps levé* with the foot held *sur le cou de pied devant*.

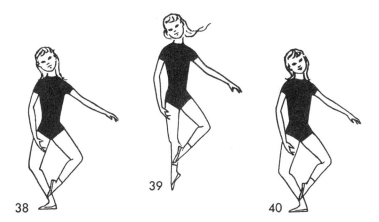

38   39   40

SOUBRESAUT (soo-breh-soh')

Soubresaut is like the *temps levé* on two feet except that it is done in Fifth Position.

41. Ready to begin. Stand in Fifth Position with the right foot front, head erect, look straight out, arms in Fifth Position Low.

42. *Demi-plié.* Count, "And."

43. Spring straight up into the air with both feet. Point strongly, cross the right foot over the left, pressing them tightly against each other. Hold your back straight and strong, your head erect, look straight out. Keep the arms in Fifth Position Low. Count, "A."

44. Come down into *demi-plié* in a good Fifth Position. The toes of both feet touch the floor at the same instant. Hold your back straight as you roll down the insteps and press your heels firmly into the floor. Count, "One."

This is the simplest form of *soubresaut*. The arms may be used in many ways in this step, but the best way for you to practice it is with the arms in Fifth Position Low.

Your teacher will teach you other ways to hold your arms as you progress in your training.

Practice this step to a 2/4 rhythm. Spring up on the preparatory beat, finish on the first beat of the measure and hold the *demi-plié* for the second beat. Practice this step 8 times with the right foot front, then 8 times with the left foot front.

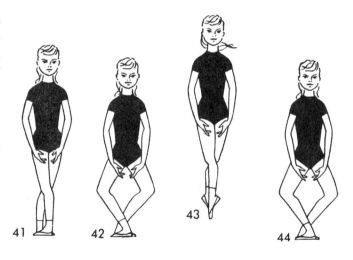

41   42   43   44

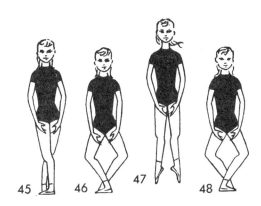

45   46   47   48

CHANGEMENT DE PIEDS
(shanzh-mahn' deh pee-ay')

Changement de pieds means "changing of the feet." This step gets its name from the fact that we begin in Fifth Position with either the right or the left foot front, spring into the air, and change the feet as we descend from the jump so that the foot that was in front finishes behind, again in Fifth Position.

45. Ready to begin. Stand in Fifth Position with right foot front, head erect, arms in Fifth Position Low. Remember to keep body well lifted out of hips and shoulder blades pulled down low as you do this step.

46. *Demi-plié.* Keep the weight equally distributed over both feet. Count, "And."

47. Spring straight up into the air, pushing down hard through the knees and toes. Press the heels forward, open the legs slightly. Count, "A."

48. As you descend from the jump, change your feet so that the left foot finishes in front of the right foot in Fifth Position. Be sure to finish in a good *demi-plié* with all of the toes and both heels firmly on the floor. Count, "One."

Practice this step to a 2/4 rhythm. Spring into the air on the preparatory beat and alight in the *plié* on the first beat of the measure. Hold the second beat in the good *plié* position. Do this 8 times, later 16 times. Remember your breath control, inhale deeply as you spring up, exhale easily as you descend.

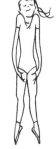

49. DON'T DO THIS. Shoulders hunched to ears on the jump.

49 ————

29

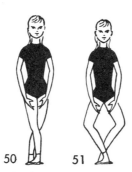

50   51   52   53   54

ÉCHAPPÉ SAUTÉ (ay-shah-pay' soh-tay')

The name of this step comes from the French verb "échapper," which means "to escape," and "sauter," which means "to jump." The legs "escape" from Fifth Position to Second Position on the jump.

50. Ready to begin. Stand in Fifth Position with the right foot front. Face directly front. Hold the head erect, the back straight, the body well lifted up out of the hips, the shoulder blades well down and under, the arms in Fifth Position Low.

51. *Demi-plié*. Remember to open the knees out over the toes, to hold the floor firmly with the big toes,

little toes, and heels, and the weight equal over both feet. Count, "And."

52. Spring straight up into the air, pulling the body up from the hips and forcing the knees and toes down very straight and pointed. The right foot is crossed over the left (*soubresaut*, page 28). As you spring up, raise the arms to Fifth Position Front and look straight front. Count, "A."

53. As you begin to descend from the jump, throw both legs apart to Second Position, keeping both knees straight and both feet pointed.

30

55

56

57

54. Finish the jump quietly in Second Position; *demi-plié*. Both arms open out to Second Position as you descend. As you alight, turn the head to the right, looking to the right side of the room. Take care not to bring the feet in toward each other as you alight, but keep the same wide Second Position you had in the air. Remember not to bend forward as you touch the floor, hold the body well up out of the hips. Press the knees back and out over the toes. Count, "One."

55. Spring straight up into the air, pointing the feet in Second Position. Count, "And."

56. As you descend from the jump bring the legs together into Fifth Position with the left foot in front of the right. Count, "A."

57. Finish in *demi-plié* in Fifth Position, left foot front. Lower the arms to Fifth Position Low as you alight and turn the head to look straight front. Count, "Two."

Practice the *échappé sauté* 8 times to a slow 2/4 rhythm, alternating right foot, then left foot, front. In the beginning it is wise to practice this step with the holding of the *plié* on the second beat of each measure so that you hold the *plié* in Second Position and the *plié* in Fifth Position each time. Later it can be practiced without this hold.

It is wise, too, to practice the feet alone without the arm or head movements until you can do the footwork correctly. Keep the arms in Fifth Position Low throughout.

When you add the arm movements, you will notice that this is the *port de bras*, which you have been practicing standing still. See *Second Steps in Ballet*. Now you can begin to understand how important it is to practice your *port de bras* so that your arms will move gracefully as you jump. Be sure that your arm movements do not become jerky because of the effort you are making with your legs and feet.

GLISSADE (glee-sahd')

The name of this step comes from the French verb "*glisser*" which means "to slide" or "to glide." There are a number of variations of *glissade*—they may be done back, front, under, over, forward, and backward. *Glissade* is in constant use in ballet as a connecting step between steps of high elevation. In this book we shall concern ourselves with the *glissade derrière* (back) and the *glissade devant* (front). Your teacher will give you other variations of the *glissade* as you progress in your training.

GLISSADE DERRIÈRE

58. Ready to begin. Stand in Fifth Position with the right foot front. Arms in Fifth Position Low, right shoulder slightly front, head inclined to right, eyes looking straight out.

59. *Demi-plié.* Be sure that the weight is evenly distributed over both feet, that the knees are pushed outward over the toes, and that your back is straight. Count, "And."

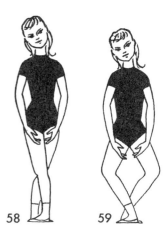

58   59

60. Slide the left foot out to a strong point in Second Position as far as the toes can reach (don't let your hips come out of alignment!). Open the arms slightly outward. Remain in the *plié* on the supporting leg. Count, "A."

61. Take a slight spring upward from the supporting foot, pointing both feet, toes grazing the floor. Open both arms outward farther to Demi-Seconde Position.

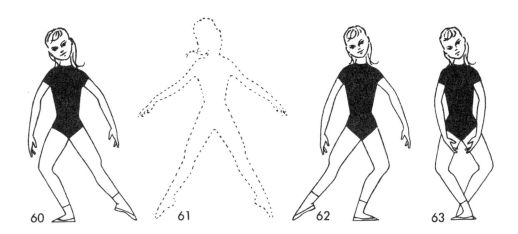

60   61   62   63

62. Transfer the weight of the body to the left foot, bending the left knee in *fondu* (roll down the foot as you *plié*). Stretch the right foot to a strong point as far as it can reach in Second Position.

63. Slide the right foot into Fifth Position in front of the left foot. Do not straighten the knees, remain in the *plié*. Close the arms to Fifth Position Low. The right shoulder remains slightly forward and the head remains inclined to the right. Count, "One."

You can tell from the musical counts that the movements illustrated in pictures 61 and 62 occur very quickly. Do not jerk them, just because they are fast. Try to make the whole thing very smooth.

Practice the *glissade* to a slow waltz (3/4 rhythm). The step should finish on the *first* beat of the measure. Take three *glissades derrière* to the left followed by one *changement* (page 29). On the *changement* turn the left shoulder slightly forward and incline the head to the left. Then repeat the whole step to the other side.

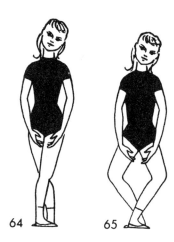

64   65

GLISSADE DEVANT

64. Ready to begin. Stand in Fifth Position with the left foot front. Arms in Fifth Position Low. Left shoulder slightly front, head inclined to the left, eyes looking straight out.

65. *Demi-plié.* Count, "And."

66. Slide the left foot out to a strong point in Second Position as far as the toes can reach. Left knee is straight, right knee remains in *plié.* Open the arms slightly outward. Count, "A."

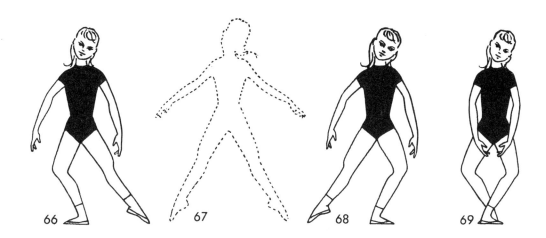

66   67   68   69

67. Take a slight spring upward through the ball of the supporting foot. Do not leave the ground but point both feet. Open both arms outward a little farther to Demi-Seconde Position.

68. Transfer the weight of the body to the left foot, bending the left knee in a soft *fondu*. Stretch the right **leg to** a strong point as far as it can reach.

69. Slide the right foot into Fifth Position behind the left foot, remaining in the *plié*. Close the arms to Fifth Position Low. The left shoulder remains slightly forward and the head remains inclined to the left. Count, "One."

Practice the *glissade devant* just as you practice the *glissade derrière*. You may also practice one *glissade* followed by one *changement* or a *jeté* or *assemblé*.   35

ASSEMBLE (ah-sahm-blay')

The name of this step comes from the French verb "*assembler,*" which means "to bring together." There are a number of variations of *assemblé*. They may be done over, under, front, behind, forward, and backward. In this book we shall concern ourselves only with the *assemblé dessus* (ah-sahm-blay' deh-sü') (over) and the *assemblé dessous* (ah-sahm-blay' deh-soo') (under). Your teacher will teach you other ways to do *assemblé* as you progress in your training.

ASSEMBLÉ DESSUS, SOUTENU

An *assemblé* is said to be "*soutenu*" (soo-teh-nü') when the *plié* is sustained for a count and the knees straightened before taking the next step.

70. Ready to begin. Stand in Fifth Position, right foot front. Face front, look straight out. Arms in Fifth Position Low.

71. *Demi-plié* and at the same time slide the left foot out to a strong point in Second Position. Keep your back straight, don't bend forward. Take care not to sit into the supporting hip or to raise the hip on the left side. Count, "And."

72. Raise the left foot slightly off the floor. Count, "A."

73. Spring straight up into the air, pushing up through the ball of the right foot. Stretch your body up out of your hips, force down through the knee and toes of your right leg, stretch the left leg into a strong point. Open the arms to Demi-Seconde Position, incline the head to the left.

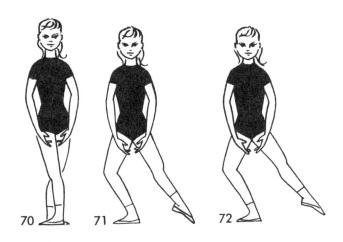

74. As you descend from the jump, bring the feet together into Fifth Position, in the air, with the left foot front.

75. Finish in *demi-plié* in Fifth Position with the left foot front. Both feet must touch the floor at the very same instant. Don't forget to roll down your insteps into the heels. Count, "One."

76. Straighten both knees as you lower both arms to Fifth Position Low. Count, "And two."

Practice this *assemblé soutenu* to a slow 3/4 rhythm. The landing from the jump should take place on the first beat of the measure and the straightening of the knees on the first beat of the following measure. Practice 8 *assemblés dessus, soutenu*, alternating left and right foot.

73   74   75   76

ASSEMBLÉ DESSOUS, SOUTENU

77. Ready to begin. Stand in Fifth Position, left foot front, head erect, look straight out, arms in Fifth Position Low.

78. *Demi-plié* and at the same time slide the left foot out to a strong point in Second Position. Count, "And."

79. Raise the left foot slightly off the floor. Count, "A."

80. Spring straight up into the air, pushing forcefully up through the ball of the right foot. Tense both legs and point both feet hard. Open the arms to Demi-Seconde Position and incline the head to the right.

81. As you descend from the jump, bring both feet together into Fifth Position with the left foot behind.

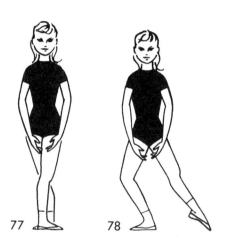

77   78

82. Finish softly in a good *demi-plié* in Fifth Position, left foot behind. Don't forget that the toes of both feet must touch the floor at the same instant. Press both heels firmly into the floor; do not roll over onto the arches as you *plié*. Count, "One."

79 80 81 82 83

83. Straighten both knees as you lower both arms to
    Fifth Position Low. Count, "And two."

Practice this *assemblé dessous* just as you practice the
assemblé dessus, alternating left and right foot. Doing 8
assemblés dessus will cause you to travel forward from the
back of the room to the front. Doing 8 *assemblés dessous*
will cause you to travel backward from the front of the
room to the back.

As you progress in your studies, you may take the *assemblé "de suite"* (deh su-eet'). That is, instead of
straightening the knees after the *assemblé* is finished, the
second *assemblé* is made from the *plié* of the first.

JETÉ (zheh-tay')

The name of this step comes from the French verb "jeter," which means "to fling." In this step we fling the leg out and then fall upon it. There are many kinds of jetés. In this book we shall concern ourselves only with the jeté derrière (in back) and the jeté devant (in front). These are also called "jeté à la seconde en avant" and "jeté à la seconde en arrière," or jeté to second position traveling forward and backward. You will learn other ways to do jeté as you progress in your training.

JETÉ DERRIÈRE

84. Ready to begin. Stand in Fifth Position, left foot front, face directly front, head erect, look straight out, arms held in Demi-Seconde Position.

85. Demi-plié and at the same time slide the right foot out to a strong point in Second Position, raising it slightly above the floor. The brush on the floor should be heard. Hold your back straight, don't bend forward. Keep the arms nicely in the Demi-Seconde Position without any strain in the hands or stiffness in the elbows. Count, "And."

86. Spring straight up into the air, forcing the left knee to straighten and the left foot to point downward.

The right knee and foot must also be straight and pointed. Count, "A."

87. Fall into a demi-plié on the right foot directly in front of the left foot. At the same time raise the left foot to a pointed position directly behind the calf of the right leg and incline the head to the right. The left foot should touch the right leg and both knees must be pushed back and out. As you fall onto the right foot, be sure to turn it out so that the heel is well forward. Remember to alight from the jump into a soft fondu—that is, roll down the instep into the heel as you plié.

40

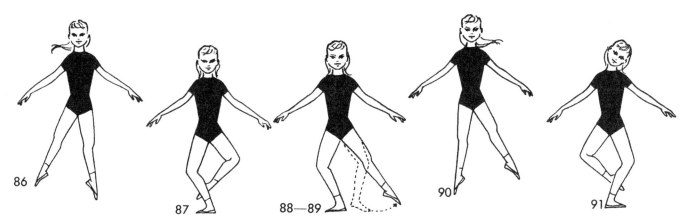

86   87   88—89   90   91

88. Repeat the *jeté* onto the left foot. Brush the left foot down and out to Second Position—touch the floor as you brush so that the sound is heard.

89. Finish the brush in a strong point in Second Position a little above the floor. Count, "And."

90. Spring straight up into the air, pushing up through the ball of the right foot; stretch the knee and the toes forcefully downward into a strong point as you lift the body up out of the hips. The left knee and foot must be straight and pointed, too. Count, "A."

91. Fall into a *demi-plié* on the left foot directly in front of the right foot; at the same time raise the right foot to a pointed position behind the calf of the left leg and incline the head to the left. Count, "Two."

Continue to practice the *jeté derrière* alternating right and left foot 8 times. This takes you in a direct line forward from the back of the room to the front. Take care that you do your brush directly to Second Position each time and that you fall directly over the supporting foot, not out to the side. Practice to a slow 2/4 rhythm, checking each landing for straight back, turned-out knees, turned-out supporting foot, heel pressed firmly into the floor, and foot straight, not rolled in on the arch.

JETÉ DEVANT

92. Ready to begin. Stand in Fifth Position, left foot front, head erect, look straight ahead, arms in Demi-Seconde Position.

93. *Demi-plié* and at the same time slide the left foot out to a strong point in Second Position, allowing it to finish slightly above the floor. The brush on the floor should be heard. Hold your back straight, don't bend forward. Count, "And."

94. Spring straight up into the air, forcing the right knee to straighten and the right foot into a strong downward point. The left knee and foot must be straight and pointed too. Count, "A."

95. Fall into a *plié* on the left foot directly behind the right foot. At the same time raise the right foot to a pointed position directly in front of the left shin and incline the head to the left. Press the knees well back

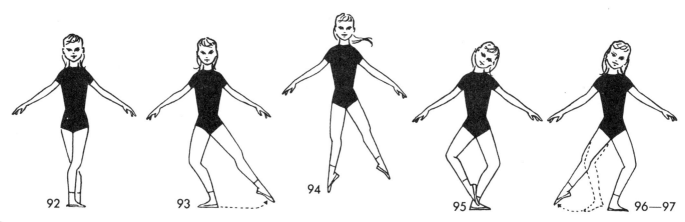

and out and hold the right foot close to the left leg. As you alight from the spring, be sure to use your instep and to press the left heel forward on the floor. Count, "One."

96. Repeat the *jeté* onto the right foot. This time brush the right foot out to Second Position from its place in front of the left leg. Slide the right foot down on the floor.

98

99

97. Point the right foot strongly in Second Position a little above the floor. Count, "And."

98. Spring straight up into the air, pushing up forcefully through the left foot into a strong point, lift the body well out of the hips, straighten the head. Count, "And."

99. Fall into a *demi-plié* on the right foot directly behind the left foot. At the same time raise the left foot to a pointed position in front of the right shin and incline the head to the right. Count, "Two."

Continue to practice the *jeté devant* alternating left and right foot. This takes you in a direct line backward. Take care not to jump to the side. Practice as in the *jeté derrière*.

In these *allegro* steps you can easily see how our exercises at the barre help to prepare us for their proper execution. For example, the *battement dégagé* helps us with the *échappé*, the *battement soutenu* is actually part of the step "assemblé," and the *battement frappé* is actually part of the step "jeté." You can begin to understand, therefore, the importance of practicing the barre exercises carefully and correctly in order to dance better.

COUPÉ (coo-pay')

The name of this step comes from the French verb "*couper*," which means "to cut." We "cut" one foot away from the other.

There are several different ways to do this step. The *coupé* may be used simply as a preparation to transfer the weight from one foot to another or it may be done as a jumping step in *allegro*. Since this book deals with *allegro* steps, we shall concern ourselves with the *coupé sauté, dessous and dessus* (coo-pay' soh-tay', deh-soo', deh-sü') (*coupé* jump, under and over).

COUPÉ DESSOUS

100. Ready to begin. Stand on the right foot with the left foot pointed behind the right heel. The body is facing *en croisé* (in this case the lower left corner of the room). Hold the right arm in Fifth Position Low, the left arm in Demi-Seconde (Cecchetti Third Position), and the head inclined to the right.

101. *Demi-plié* and raise the left foot to a pointed position in back of the right calf muscle. Count, "And."

102. Spring up through the ball of the right foot, pointing the toes hard. Count, "A."

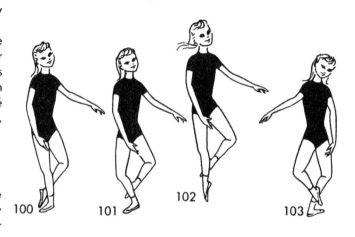

103. Fall onto the left foot directly under the right, rolling down the instep into a good *demi-plié*. At the same time raise the right foot to a pointed position in front of the left shin. As you descend, reverse the positions of the arms so that the left arm is in Fifth Position Low, the right in Demi-Seconde, and the head inclined to the left. Count, "One, two."

44

COUPÉ DESSUS

104. From the position in which you have landed after taking the *coupé dessous* spring up through the ball of the left foot.

105. Fall onto the right foot directly over the left foot. At the same time raise the left leg to a pointed position behind the calf muscle of the right leg. As you descend, reverse the positions of the arms and head so that the right arm is in Fifth Position Low, the left in Demi-Seconde, and the head inclined to the right. Count, "Three, four."

In doing these *coupés* be sure that your knees and your supporting foot are well turned out and that you are not rolling in on your insteps in the *demi-pliés*.

Practice the *coupé*, alternating *dessous* and *dessus*, to a slow 4/4 rhythm. This is valuable practice to develop the springiness of your insteps, if you work carefully and correctly, and will develop strength in your insteps and ankles as well as good *ballon*. Take 6 *coupés* alternating *dessous* and *dessus*, finish with an *assemblé dessus*, *soutenu* (page 36). On the *assemblé* turn to face the opposite corner. Then repeat the *coupés* and the *assemblé* to the other side.

PAS DE CHAT (pah deh shah')

Pas de chat in French means "step of the cat." It gets its name from the swift action of the feet like a cat's paws when it pounces upon something. *Pas de chat* may be done *petit* (small) or *grand* (big). In doing *petit pas de chat* the feet are raised only to ankle height. In doing *grand pas de chat* the feet are raised to knee height. In this book we shall concern ourselves with the *grand pas de chat*, as the *petit pas de chat* is more difficult because it requires more speed.

106. Ready to begin. Stand in Fifth Position, right foot front. Face directly front with the head erect and the arms in Fifth Position Low.

107. *Demi-plié* with the right leg and at the same time raise the left knee so that the left foot points behind the right knee. As you do this, raise the arms to Fourth Position Front with the left arm across the body and bend the body a little to the left side, turning the head left to look at the left knee. Count, "And."

108. Spring up into the air, raising the right knee. Be sure that both knees are well turned out and both feet pointed.

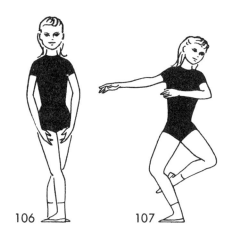

106   107

109. Alight on the left foot, rolling down the instep into a good *demi-plié*, with the right foot strongly pointed in front of the left knee. The body remains bent to the left. Count, "A."

110. Quickly follow the left foot with the right, closing it to Fifth Position in front of the left, and remain in the *demi-plié*. Do not change the position of your body or head. Count, "One."

108

109

110

As in all *allegro* steps take care that in alighting from the jump you do not allow your knees to fall in front of your insteps so that the arches are rolled under. Be sure that your knees are well turned out and pressed as far back as possible all through this step.

Practice the *pas de chat* to a slow 2/4 rhythm. Take 3 *pas de chat* to the left, followed by 1 *changement* (page 29). On the *changement* lower both arms to Fifth Position Low and face directly front. Then begin the *pas de chat* to the other side.

111. DON'T DO THIS!

111

PAS DE BASQUE, GLISSÉ
(pah deh bahsk, glee-say')

Pas de basque gets its name from the Basque country, where France and Spain meet. "*Pas*" means "step"— step of the Basques. The *pas de basque* is a basic step of the folk dancing of these peoples. In ballet it has been adopted to be performed in two ways—"*glissé*," or sliding on the floor, and "*sauté*," or jumping off the floor. In this book we are concerned with the *pas de basque glissé*. The *pas de basque* may be performed *en avant* (forward) and *en arrière* (backward).

PAS DE BASQUE, en avant

112. Ready to begin. Stand in Fifth Position with left foot front. Direction of the body is *en croisé* (here the lower right corner of the room). Hold arms in Fifth Position Low and head inclined to right.

113. *Demi-plié* with the right leg and slide the left foot front to a strong point in Fourth Position. Raise the arms to Second Position; the head remains inclined to the right. Count, "And."

114. Describe a *demi-rond de jambe à terre*; finish with left foot strongly pointed to Second Position. Remain in *demi-plié* on right leg. Straighten head.

112 113 114

115. Transfer the weight from the right foot to the left with a little spring. At the same time incline the head to the left. Count, "One."

116. Slide right foot into First Position, bending knee as foot slides in. Lower arms to Fifth Position Low with head remaining inclined to left. The weight is now equalized over both feet. Count, "And."

117. Continue to slide the right foot, passing through Fifth Position, to Fourth Position *en croisé*. Keep

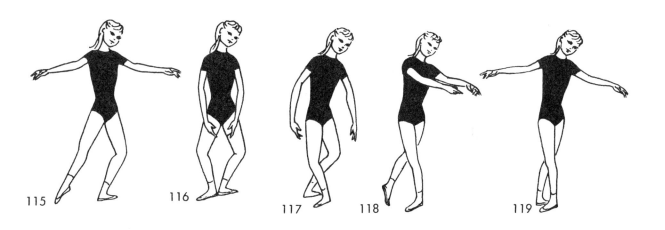

the weight equalized over both feet, both heels pressed firmly on the floor, both knees bent in *demi-plié*. Bend body to left and raise arms a little.

118. Transfer weight to right foot, straightening both knees and pointing left foot strongly in *croisé derrière* position. At the same time raise both arms to Fifth Position Front, body still inclined to left. Take care that both legs are well turned out from the hips, that the heel of the right foot is pressed forward, and that you point on the inside of the big left toe with heel pressed down. Count, "Two."

119. Close the left foot behind the right into Fifth Position *demi-plié*. At the same time open both arms to Second Position. The body and head remain inclined to the left. Count, "And three."

Practice the *pas de basque en avant* to a slow 3/4 rhythm (mazurka is excellent). Alternate left and right 8 times.

49

PAS DE BASQUE, en arrière

120. Ready to begin. Stand in Fifth Position facing straight front, right foot front. Arms in Fifth Position Low, head inclined to the right.

121. *Demi-plié* with the right leg and slide the left foot to a strong point in second, open both arms to Second Position. Count, "And."

122. Transfer the weight from the right foot to the left by springing up through the ball of the right foot till both feet point, just grazing the floor, and then rolling down the left foot through the instep into a *demi-plié* with the heel pressed firmly into the floor. The right leg should be extended with straight knee to a strong point in Second Position. Head remains inclined to the right and the arms in Second Position. Count, "One."

123. Slide the right foot into First Position, bending the right knee as the foot slides in. Lower the arms to Fifth Position Low; head remains inclined to the right.

124. Continue to slide the right foot back to Fourth Position *en croisé* with the weight equalized over both feet, bend the body to the right side with the head remaining inclined to the right, raise the arms a little. Count, "And."

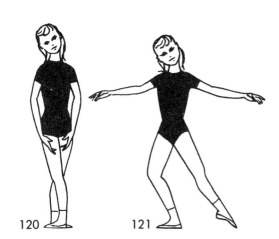

120   121

125. Step back onto the right foot, pointing the left foot to *croisé devant*. Raise both arms to Fifth Position Front; head and body remain inclined to the right. Count, "Two."

126. Close the left foot into Fifth Position, *demi-plié*, in front of the right foot. Open both arms to Second Position, inclining the head and the body to the left side. Count, "And three."

Practice the *pas de basque en arrière* 8 times alternating left and right.

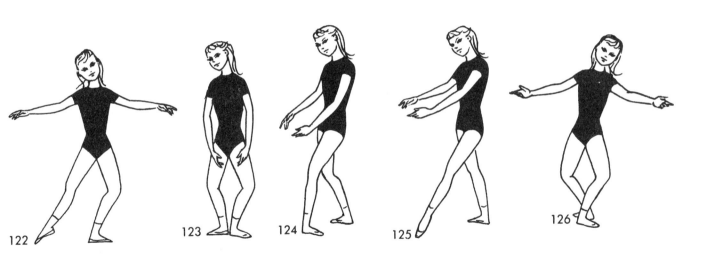

CHASSÉ (shah-say')

This step gets its name from the French verb "chasser," which means "to chase." We "chase" one foot with the other. Chassé may be done forward, backward, or sideward and in any of the body positions.

In this book we shall concern ourselves only with the chassé en avant (chassé traveling forward). The direction of the body is effacé with the arms held in Demi-Seconde, as this is the simplest form in which to learn this step.

CHASSÉ, en avant

Ready to begin. Stand in Fifth Position, left foot front, facing in the direction effacé (in this case the lower left corner of the room). Arms in Demi-Seconde Position, head inclined to the right.

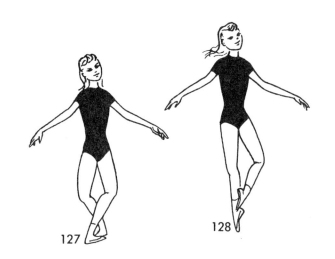

127. *Demi-plié* with the weight equal over both feet. Count, "And."

128. Spring straight up into the air, raising the left foot to point in front of the right ankle.

129. Alight on the right foot in *demi-plié* with the left foot pointed in front of the right instep.

130. Slide the left foot forward, throwing the weight of the body upon it, until the right leg is stretched into a strong point behind. Count, "One."

131. Draw the right foot quickly up behind the left, springing into the air with the feet pointed strongly and pressed tightly together in Fifth Position. Count, "And."

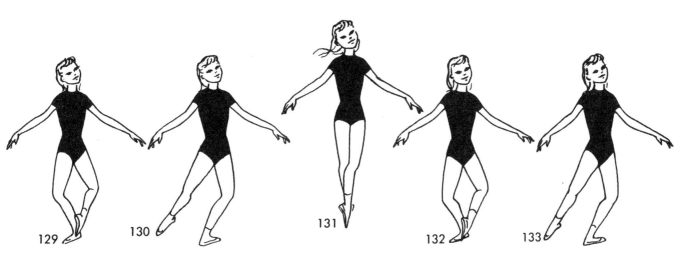

129 130 131 132 133

132. Alight on the right foot in *demi-plié* with the left foot pointed in front of the right instep.

133. Slide the left foot forward, throwing the weight of the body upon it, until the right leg is stretched into a strong point behind. Count, "Two."

Continue to practice the *chassé*, in this manner, traveling forward in a diagonal line from the upper right corner of the room to the lower left corner.

You will notice that the knees are kept straight during the jump into the air the second time. The only time the front knee bends in the air is the first time. This is as a preparation for a series of *chassés*. For all succeeding *chassés* keep both knees straight in the air.

Practice to a 6/8 rhythm played slowly so that you may think about getting everything correct. Reverse the direction of the body and practice the *chassé* the same way with the right foot front.

PAS DE BOURRÉE (pah deh boo-ray')

This step gets its name from a famous dance of the eighteenth century. The bourrée was the native dance of Auvergne, a province of France. Later this dance was adopted by the French Court. Its basic step was then adopted for use by the ballet and is known as "pas de bourrée," or "step of the bourrée."

There are many variations of pas de bourrée. They may be done over, under, front, back, turning, changing, and without changing. In this book we concern ourselves with pas de bourrée dessous (under) and pas de bourrée dessus (over).

The pas de bourrée is described in this book as it is performed in my school, the School of Ballet Repertory in New York City. Here it is performed with a fondu (plié) on the second step. This is an old traditional way of performing this step and I prefer it because it gives great lightness to the step as well as smoothness. Practicing it in this manner develops excellent control of the feet and insteps. If this is different than the way your teacher teaches it, do not worry over it but try to learn it both ways.

PAS DE BOURRÉE DESSOUS

134. Ready to begin. Stand in Fifth Position, left foot front, left shoulder slightly front, head inclined to the left, and the arms in Fifth Position Low.

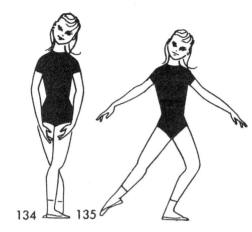

134   135

135. Demi-plié and slide the right foot out to a strong point in Second Position slightly above the floor. At the same time raise both arms to Demi-Seconde Position. (Back straight, shoulder pulled down, body well lifted out of hips!) Count, "And."

136. Rise up on the demi-pointe of the left foot and at the same time bring the right foot into Fifth Position on the demi-pointe behind the left with both knees pulled up tight. Count, "One."

136   137   138   139

137. Step to Second Position on the *demi-pointe* with the left foot so that you are standing with the weight equal over both feet. Bring the head erect, look straight front.

138. Lower the left heel to the floor in *demi-plié*. At the same time stretch the right leg into a strong point in Second Position, toes touching the floor. Lower the arms slightly. This action takes place at the instant that you step on the foot in Second Position. Count, "And."

139. Slide the right foot into Fifth Position in front of the left foot. Remain in the *plié*. Bring the right shoulder slightly forward and incline the head to the right as the foot slides in. Count, "Two."

Do not straighten the knees before beginning the *pas de bourrée* to the other side; *dégagé* the left foot *à la seconde* while remaining in the *plié*.

Practice the *pas de bourrée* alternating right and left. If you practice with music, use a slow 4/4 rhythm, count, "And one, and two, and three, and four." The preparatory brush then is done on count "Four."

PAS DE BOURRÉE DESSUS

The *pas de bourrée dessus* differs from the *pas de bourrée dessous* in that the foot crosses over in the front rather than under in the back.

140. Ready to begin. Stand in Fifth Position with the right foot front, right shoulder slightly front, head inclined to the right, and the arms in Fifth Position Low.

141. *Demi-plié* and slide the right foot out to a strong point in Second Position slightly above the floor. At the same time raise both arms to Demi-Seconde Position. Remember that you must not permit the knee to fall in front of the arch; press it back over the toes. Count, "And."

142. Rise up on the *demi-pointe* of the left foot and at the same time bring the right foot into Fifth Position on the *demi-pointe* in front of the left. Pull both knees up tight. Count, "One."

143. Step to Second Position on the *demi-pointe* with the left foot. Bring the head erect and look straight out.

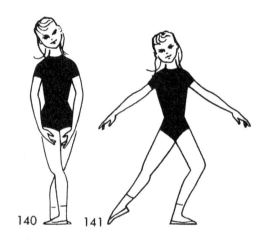

140   141

144. Lower the left heel to the ground in *plié*. At the same time stretch the right leg to a strong point in Second Position, toes touching the floor, and lower the arms a little. This action takes place at the instant you step to Second Position. Count, "And."

56

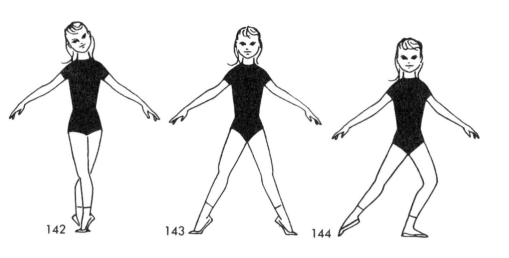

142   143   144   145

145. Slide the right foot into Fifth Position in back of the
       left, remaining in the *plié*. Bring the left shoulder
       slightly forward and incline the head to the left;
       lower the arms to Fifth Position Low. Count, "Two."
           Practice the *pas de bourrée dessus* the same way you
       practice the *pas de bourrée dessous*, alternating right
       and left.

BALANCÉ (bah-lahn-say')

This step gets its name from the French verb "balancer," which means "to sway." In this step we may sway from side to side or from front to back. We shall practice it from side to side.

146. Ready to begin. Stand in Fifth Position with the right foot front, face front, head erect, looking straight out. Arms in Fifth Position Low.

147. *Demi-plié* and slide the left foot out to a strong point in Second Position a little above the floor. Raise both arms to Fifth Position Front.

148. Transfer the weight to the left foot with a little spring by using your insteps (push up through the right foot, roll down through the left foot) falling into a *demi-plié*. Open both arms halfway out to Second Position. Count, "One."

149. Bring the right foot behind the left foot slightly off the floor.

150. Transfer the weight to the ball of the right foot, straightening the right knee and lifting the left foot very slightly off the floor. Count, "Two."

151. Fall on the left foot, rolling down the instep into a *demi-plié*, and raise the right foot very slightly off the floor behind the left foot. At the same time lower the arms to Fifth Position Low. Count, "Three."

Repeat the three counts to the right side. Practice the

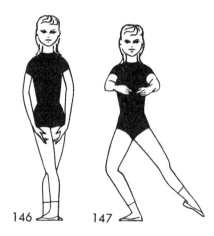

146   147

balancé to a slow waltz (3/4 rhythm). Alternate left and right 16 times. Practice it holding the arms in Fifth Position Low, until you have the feet well under control, then add the *port de bras*. Your teacher will teach you other ways to use the arms as you progress in your training.

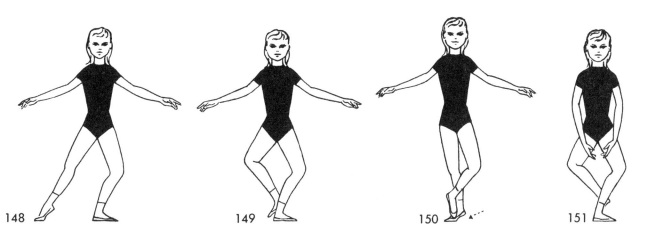

148   149   150   151

SISSONNE (FERMÉ) (see-sohn' fehr-may')

This step gets its name from the dancer who invented it. There are many different kinds of *sissonnes*. They may be done closed, open, over, under, changing, without changing, forward, backward, and sideward. They may be done in any of the body positions such as *croisé*, *écarté*, and *effacé*, in any of the *arabesque* positions, and with a variety of *port de bras*. In the Russian school the *temps levé* from two feet to one foot (page 24) is called a *"sissonne simple."*

We are concerned with the *sissonne fermé*, *en avant* and *en arrière* (*sissonne* closed, forward and backward). These may be done traveling from the back of the room to the front and vice versa, or they may be taken traveling on a diagonal line from corner to corner.

SISSONNE FERMÉ, en avant

The *sissonne fermé*, *en avant*, is here described taken on a diagonal line from the upper right corner of the room to the lower left corner (direction is *effacé*) with the arms in the First Arabesque position.

152. Ready to begin. Stand in Fifth Position with the left foot front. Face the lower left corner of the room. Head erect, look straight ahead, arms in Fifth Position Low.

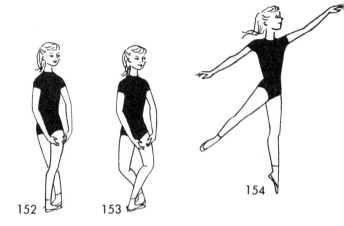

152   153   154

153. *Demi-plié* with both legs.

154. Spring forward into the air, taking the right leg back to Fourth Position in the air, point both feet strongly, and force both knees to straighten. At the same time open both arms outward. Count, "And."

155. Alight softly on the left foot in *fondu* (roll down the instep into a *plié*) with the arms in First Arabesque

155   156   157

158

158. DON'T DO THIS! In practicing this step take great care that your body does not bend forward (break) as you alight from the spring. You must keep a good lift out of the hips and with the ribs, both in the air and on the floor, otherwise the step will give the appearance of being labored and heavy instead of easy and light.

position. Hold the good lift out of the hips and keep your back straight and strong with the shoulder blades well pulled down. Count, "A."

156. Touch the floor in Fourth Position Back with the toes of the right foot.

157. Slide the right foot into Fifth Position behind the left, maintaining the *plié*. Lower the arms to Fifth Position Low. Count, "One."

Practice 8 *sissonnes* in this manner, traveling always toward the lower left corner. Then repeat on the other foot, traveling on the diagonal from the upper left corner to the lower right. Practice to a slow waltz (3/4) rhythm. The closing after the spring takes place on the *first* beat of the measure and the second two beats are held in the *plié* position. The next *sissonne* takes its spring from this *plié*. You may practice this step with the arms held in Fifth Position Low until you have control of the feet and legs. You may also practice it with the arms held in First Arabesque position throughout without raising and lowering them each time. As you progress in your studies, add the *port de bras*.

61

SISSONNE FERMÉ, en arrière

The *sissonne fermé, en arrière*, is here described taken on a diagonal line from the lower right corner to the upper left (direction *effacé*) with the arms in *effacé* position.

159. Ready to begin. Stand in Fifth Position with the right foot front. Face the lower right corner of the room. Head erect, look straight ahead. Arms in Fifth Position Low.

160. *Demi-plié* with both legs and raise the arms to Fifth Position in front.

161. Spring backward, taking the right leg front to Fourth Position in the air, and open the arms to Third Position with the left arm up. At the same time incline the head to the left and look out to the audience. Point both feet strongly and force both knees to straighten. Count, "And."

162. Come down softly on the left foot in *fondu* (roll down into a *demi-plié*), maintaining the *effacé* position of the arms and head.

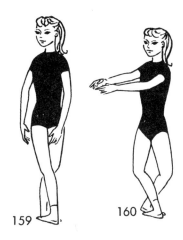

159.   160.

163. Touch the floor with the toes of your right foot.

164. Slide the right foot into Fifth Position in front of the left foot, maintaining the *plié*. The arms and head remain in the *effacé* position. Count, "One."

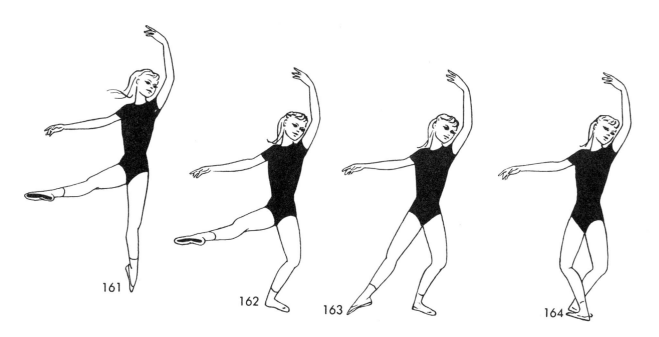

161

162

163

164

Practice this step exactly as I have described the practice for the *sissonne* traveling forward. Maintain the arms in the *effacé* position throughout once you have raised them to this position. For preliminary practice it is wise not to use the arms but to maintain them in the Fifth Position Low until you have acquired the necessary skill with the legs and feet.

Take care that you do not allow the open leg to fly up too high as you alight from the spring, but maintain strong control of your hips and back.